Bayview Ave. School

A
LITTLE
JAMIE
BOOK

What It's Like to Be
Qué se siente al ser

RYAN HOWARD

BY
JOE RASEMAS
AND
PATRICE SHERMAN

TRANSLATED BY
EIDA DE LA VEGA

Mitchell Lane

PUBLISHERS
P.O. Box 196
Hockessin, Delaware 19707
Visit us on the web: www.mitchelllane.com
Comments? email us:
mitchelllane@mitchelllane.com

LITTLE JAMIE BOOKS

What It's Like to Be . . .   Qué se siente al ser . . .

The Jonas Brothers/Los Hermanos Jonas
Miley Cyrus
President Barack Obama/El Presidente Barack Obama
Ryan Howard

Library of Congress Cataloging-in-Publication Data
Rasemas, Joe.
  What it's like to be Ryan Howard = Qué se siente al ser Ryan Howard / by Joe Rasemas and Patrice
Sherman; translated by Eida de la Vega.
    p. cm. — (What it's like to be/A Little Jamie books)
  Includes bibliographical references and index.
  ISBN 978-1-58415-845-5 (library bound)
1. Howard, Ryan, 1979– — Juvenile literature. 2. Baseball players — United States — Biography — Juvenile
literature. I. Sherman, Patrice. II. Vega, Eida de la. III. Title. IV. Title: Qué se siente al ser Ryan Howard.
  GV865.H67R37 2009
  796.357092 — dc22
  [B]
                                                                        2009019618

ABOUT THE AUTHORS: Pat Sherman lives and writes in Cambridge, Massachusetts, near the city
of Boston. She is a Red Sox fan, but when she she visits her sister in Pennsylvania, she likes to root for
the Phillies, too.
    Children's book illustrator Joe Rasemas is a lifelong Phillies fan. He lives near Philadelphia with his
wife, Cynthia, and son, Jeremy.

ACERCA DE LOS AUTORES: Pat Sherman vive y escribe en Cambridge, Massachusetts, cerca de la
ciudad de Boston. Es aficionada a los Medias Rojas, pero cuando visita a su hermana en Pensilvania,
le gusta apoyar a los Filis.
    El ilustrador de libros infantiles, Joe Rasemas, ha sido aficionado a los Filis toda su vida. Vive cerca
de Filadelfia con su esposa, Cynthia, y su hijo, Jeremy.

ABOUT THE TRANSLATOR: Eida de la Vega was born in Havana, Cuba, and now lives in New
Jersey with her mother, her husband — who likes any baseball team that offers a good game — and her
two children. Eida has worked at Lectorum/Scholastic, and as editor of the magazine Selecciones del
Reader's Digest.

ACERCA DE LA TRADUCTORA: Eida de la Vega nació en La Habana, Cuba, y ahora vive en
Nueva Jersey con su madre, su esposo — al que le gusta cualquier equipo de béisbol que ofrezca un
buen partido — y sus dos hijos. Ha trabajado en Lectorum/Scholastic y, como editora, en la revista
Selecciones del Reader's Digest.

What It's Like to Be/
Qué se siente al ser

RYAN HOWARD

4

Ryan Howard plays baseball for the Philadelphia Phillies. He's been hitting home runs since he was in the Little League. He hit an amazing 430-foot home run when he was only 12. He still hits a lot of home runs. And that takes a lot of practice.

Ryan Howard juega béisbol para los Filis de Filadelfia. Ha estado pegando jonrones desde que estaba en las Ligas Pequeñas. Cuando tenía 12 años, conectó un tremendo jonrón de 430 pies. Todavía batea muchos jonrones y eso requiere mucha práctica.

Ryan gets up around 7:30 every morning. He knows how important healthy food is, so he eats a lot of protein like eggs and lean meat, along with fresh fruit for breakfast. (But sometimes he has a bowl of his favorite cereal—Cocoa Puffs™!)

Ryan se levanta todos los días alrededor de las 7:30 de la mañana. Como sabe lo importante que es la comida saludable, en el desayuno come muchas proteínas, como huevos y carne sin grasa, y también frutas frescas. (Pero en ocasiones se come un bol de su cereal preferido: Cocoa Puffs™.)

After breakfast, he works out at the gym. First he stretches. Stretching keeps his muscles loose so that he can swing the bat all the way around. Then he lifts weights to keep his arms and shoulders strong, which helps him hit the ball hard. After lifting weights, he jogs. Jogging keeps him fast so that he can round all the bases.

RYAN'S SHOES
(ZAPATOS)
SIZE 15

Después del desayuno, entrena en el gimnasio. Primero hace estiramientos para mantener los músculos relajados, y así poder hacer un *swing* completo cuando batea. Luego, levanta pesas para tener brazos y hombros fuertes, y poder pegarle con fuerza a la pelota. Después de levantar pesas, trota para adquirir velocidad y poder correr todas las bases.

Ryan plays first base, and every day he works with his coach, Sam Perlozzo. He practices catching ground balls and throwing runners out. Before the 2009 season, he lost 25 pounds to help make him quicker.

Ryan juega la primera base. Todos los días trabaja con su entrenador, Sam Perlozzo. Practica cómo agarrar las pelotas y tirarlas rápidamente para sacar al lanzador en *out*. Antes de la temporada del 2009, Ryan perdió 25 libras para poder ser más rápido.

SAM

In the afternoon, it's time for batting practice. Ryan once hit the longest home run in Citizens Bank Park history. The ball traveled 505 feet. How far is that? A train car is nearly 50 feet long, so 505 feet is longer than a ten-car train!

Por las tardes, toca práctica de bateo. Una vez, Ryan bateó el jonrón más largo en la historia de Citizens Bank Park. La pelota viajó 505 pies. ¿Cuán lejos es eso? Un vagón de tren mide casi 50 pies de largo, de modo que 505 pies equivaldría a un poco más del largo de un tren de diez vagones.

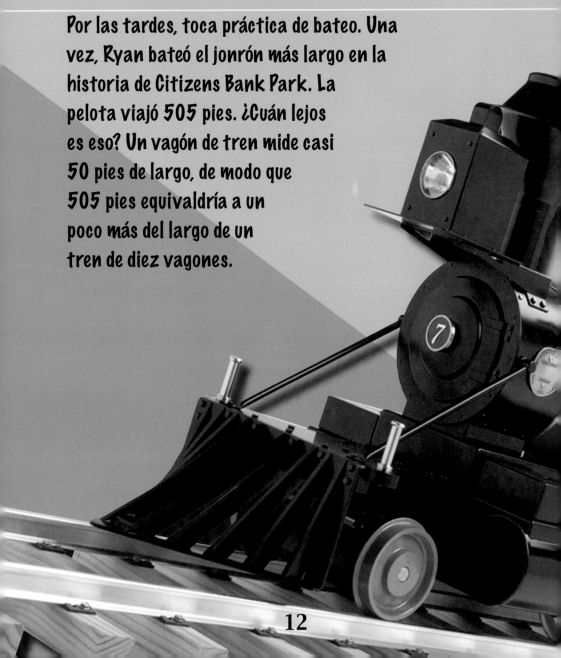

HOWARD EXPRESS

Ryan finds time to share a laugh with his close
friend, Phillies shortstop Jimmy Rollins.
Jimmy invited Ryan to live with him
when Ryan was a rookie.

Ryan siempre encuentra tiempo para
divertirse con su buen amigo, el campocorto
de los Filis, Jimmy Rollins. Cuando Ryan era
un novato, Jimmy le dijo que podía venir a vivir
a su casa.

14

MICROPHONE

There are always reporters
waiting to get an interview with Ryan,
so he also finds time to answer all their questions.

Siempre hay periodistas esperando para entrevistar
a Ryan, así que también dedica un tiempo a
contestar todas sus preguntas.

A lot of fans come to see Ryan practice. After practice, he goes to the fence and signs autographs. He signs balls, bats, sneakers, hats, baseball gloves, and other items for his fans.

Muchos aficionados van a ver entrenar a Ryan. Después de la práctica, Ryan va hasta la cerca y firma autógrafos. Firma pelotas, bates, zapatillas deportivas, gorras, guantes de béisbol y otros objetos que sus admiradores le piden que firme.

Back in the clubhouse, Ryan chats with the Phillies manager, Charlie Manuel, about the team they'll be facing. He views videotapes of the opposing pitcher, and squeezes in some fun by playing a video game or two with Jimmy. His favorites are *Contra* and *MLB The Show*.

De regreso a las oficinas del equipo, Ryan conversa con el gerente de los Filis, Charlie Manuel, acerca del equipo contra el que van a jugar. Mira videos del lanzador contrario, y hasta encuentra tiempo para disfrutar uno o dos juegos de video con Jimmy. Sus preferidos son *Contra* y *MLB The Show*.

CHARLIE

The time comes to take the field. The announcer introduces the players one by one. The game is about to start!

Llega
la hora de salir
al campo. El locutor
presenta a los jugadores
uno por uno. ¡El juego está a
punto de empezar!

Soon a giant American flag is stretched out on the field for the playing of the national anthem.

Enseguida, una bandera estadounidense gigante se despliega en el campo, para que se cante el himno nacional.

Ryan stands in the on-deck circle and watches teammate Chase Utley bat. From there he can study the pitcher and see what kinds of pitches he's about to face.

Ryan se para en el círculo de espera y observa batear a su compañero, Chase Utley. Desde allí puede estudiar al lanzador y ver qué tipo de lanzamientos está a punto de enfrentar.

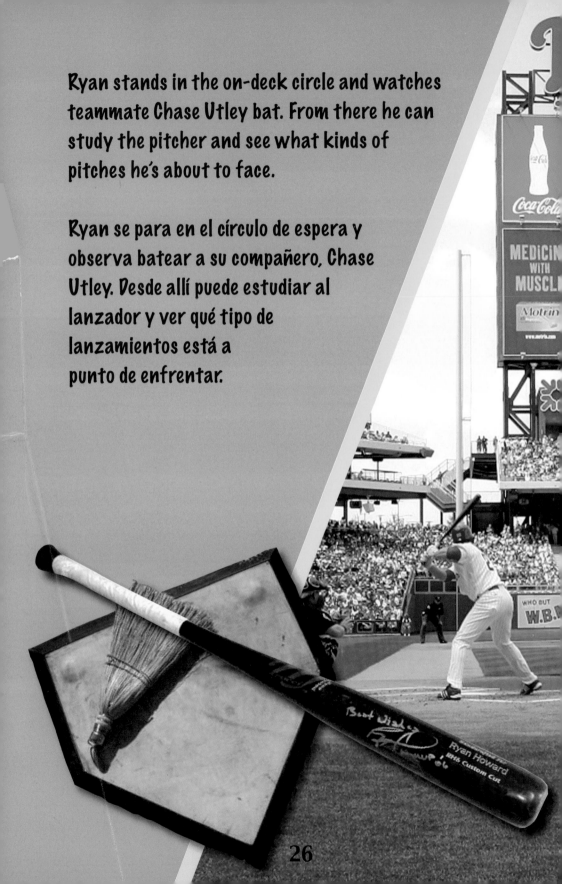

Time to bat!
Ryan hits more home runs
per at-bat than any other Major
League Baseball player.

¡Llegó la hora de batear! Ryan
conecta más jonrones por
veces al bate que ningún
otro jugador de
Grandes Ligas.

CRAACK!!!

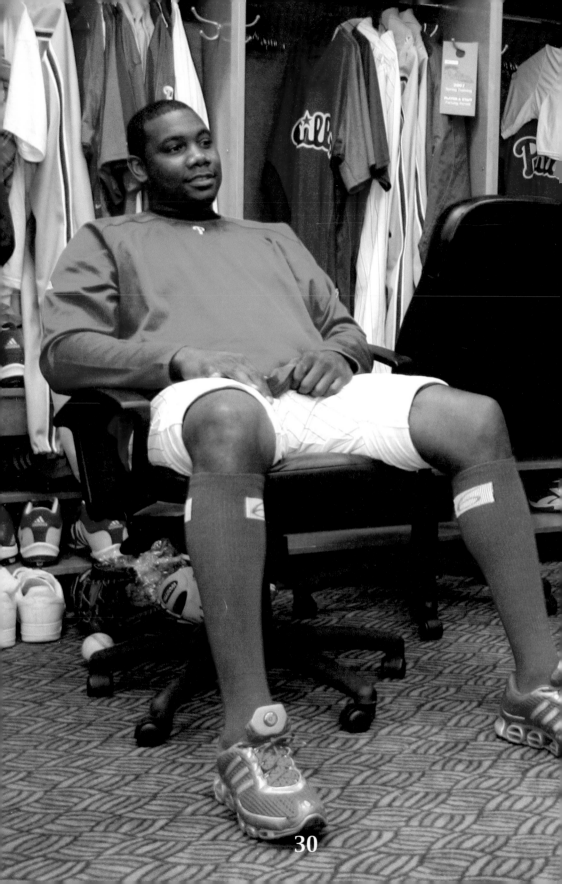

Before long, the game is over, and Ryan has helped his team win another close game. Once again, Ryan is on the star-of-the-game show, where he always seems to be asked the same question ...

"What's it like to be Ryan Howard?"

El juego ha terminado, y Ryan ha ayudado a su equipo a ganar otro partido reñido. Una vez más, Ryan es una de las estrellas entrevistadas, donde siempre parece que le hacen la misma pregunta ...

¿Qué se siente al ser Ryan Howard?

Works Consulted/Obras consultadas

Berlinicke, Jeff. "Phillies Slugger Ryan Howard: Doing Whatever It Takes to Get Job Done." *Baseball Digest,* August 2006.

Deveney, Sean. "Being Ryan Howard." *Sporting News,* April 2, 2007.

Dubois, Lou. "Tower of Power. World Champions: Philadelphia Phillies." *Sports Illustrated,* November 5, 2008.

Greenberg, Steve. "You Don't Know Ryan Howard Like I Know Ryan Howard." *Sporting News,* February 2, 2009.

Lidz, Franz. "Listen to His Bat." *Sports Illustrated,* September 18, 2006.

"Phillies—Ryan Howard Says His Only Concern Is Being in Shape." *Philadelphia Daily News,* February 16, 2008.

"Ryan Howard Answers 10 Questions." *Time,* March 23, 2009.

"Ryan Howard Emerges as Highly Marketable Star." *St. Louis Post-Dispatch,* June 26, 2007.

Ryan Howard, YouTube http://www.youtube.com/watch?v=MD6UZypo7nY&feature=related

Santoliquito, Joseph. "Howard Makes a Memory: Lefty Slugger Hits Longest Home Run in Citizens Bank Park." MLB.com, April 23, 2006.

Scarr, Mike. "Ryan Howard Big Basher the Smallest Man in Family." *Pennant Traces,* MLB.com http://mlb.mlb.com/mlb/news/postseason/traces.jsp?loc=traces_howard

Segura, Melissa. "Fantastic Phillie: Ryan Howard." *Sports Illustrated Kids,* May 2007.

Sokolove, Michael. "Ryan Howard, No Asterisk." *New York Times,* March 4, 2007. http://www.nytimes.com/2007/03/04/sports/playmagazine/04play-howard.html?_r=1

On the Internet

Major League Baseball, Official Site
http://mlb.mlb.com/index.jsp

Ryan Howard's Weplay page
http://www.weplay.com/users/RyanHoward

En Internet

Fox Sports en Español
http://msn.foxsports.com/fse/beisbol

Las Grandes Ligas de Beisbol
www.lasmayores.com

INDEX/ÍNDICE